ideals
MOTHER'S DAY

More Than 50 Years of Celebrating Life's Most Treasur

Vol. 57, No. 2

*It was a pleasure to live
on that bright and happy May morning!*
—Henry Wadsworth Longfellow

IDEALS—Vol. 57, No. 2 March MM IDEALS (ISSN 0019-137X)
is published six times a year: January, March, May, July, September, and November by
IDEALS PUBLICATIONS INCORPORATED,
535 Metroplex Drive, Suite 250, Nashville, TN 37211.
Periodical postage paid at Nashville, Tennessee, and additional mailing offices.
Copyright © MM by IDEALS PUBLICATIONS INCORPORATED.
POSTMASTER: Send address changes to Ideals, PO Box 305300,
Nashville, TN 37230. All rights reserved.

Title IDEALS registered U.S. Patent Office.
SINGLE ISSUE—U.S. $5.95 USD; Higher in Canada
ONE-YEAR SUBSCRIPTION—U.S. $19.95 USD; Canada $36.00 CDN (incl. GST and shipping); Foreign $25.95 USD
TWO-YEAR SUBSCRIPTION—U.S. $35.95 USD; Canada $66.50 CDN (incl. GST and shipping); Foreign $47.95 USD

Subscribers may call customer service at 1-800-558-4343 to make address changes.
Unsolicited manuscripts will not be returned without a self-addressed, stamped envelope.

ISBN 0-8249-1160-1   GST 131903775

Visit *Ideals*'s website at www.idealspublications.com

Cover Photo
Spring in the garden
Nancy Matthews,
photographer

Inside Front Cover
SHE LOOKS AND LOOKS, AND
STILL WITH NEW DELIGHT
Artist, James John Hill
Christie's Images/Superstock

Inside Back Cover
ON THE DUNES
Artist, Percy Lancaster
Christie's Images

IN EARLY MAY

Bliss Carman

O my dear, the world today
Is more lovely than a dream!
Magic hints from far away
Haunt the woodland, and the stream
Murmurs in his rocky bed
Things that never can be said.
Starry dogwood is in flower,
Gleaming through the mystic woods.
It is beauty's perfect hour
In the wild spring solitudes.
Now the orchards in full blow
Shed their petals white as snow.
All the air is honey-sweet
With the lilacs white and red,
Where the blossoming branches meet
In an arbor overhead;
And the laden cherry trees
Murmur with the hum of bees.
All the earth is fairy green
And the sunlight filmy gold,
Full of ecstasies unseen,
Full of mysteries untold.
Who would not be out-of-door,
Now the spring is here once more!

*A garland of dogwood blossoms adorns a field in
Louisville, Kentucky. Photo by Daniel Dempster.*

As the Heart Remembers Spring

Betty W. Stoffel

Some will be remembered
For the fortunes of their fame,
And some will be remembered
For the naming of a name.

But you will be remembered
As the heart remembers spring,
As the mind remembers beauty,
And the soul each lovely thing.

You have been skies of April
And fragrant breath of May,
And like the season's coming,
Warm-spirited and gay.

You have given freely
Of the beauty of your heart,
And you have made of friendship
Not a gesture but an art.

You have been as selfless
In the gracious things you do
As the sun that shares its kisses,
As the night that shares its dew.

You have planted roses
In lives that lay so bare;
You have sown encouragement
To those who knew despair.

By spirit's inner beauty
In every lovely thing,
You will be remembered
As the heart remembers spring!

Right: A gardener in Eugene, Oregon, uses climbing roses to send a loving message. Photo by Dennis Frates.

Overleaf: A formal Italian garden welcomes strollers in Richmond, Virginia. Photo by Gene Ahrens.

As Long as There's a Spring

Lon Myruski

Come hear the blissful harmonies
Bespreading hill and dale,
Where cadences of crickets
And peeping frogs prevail.
Where warblers and redbreasts tune
To everyone's heartstrings—
The world will never want for song
As long as there's a spring.
Come see romantic gardens mid
A blossom-scented breeze,
Where stands of blushing pinks enjoy
The kiss of honeybees.
Where arm in arm young couples stroll
Bestirred by Cupid's sting—
There'll never be an end to love
As long as there's a spring.

Enough

Mildred Fowler Field

It is enough to know that somewhere
   springtime
Has dipped a brush in green and splashed
   the trees.
It is enough to know that somewhere
   bluebirds
Are singing their ecstatic melodies.
It is enough to know that somewhere petals
Will drift across the grass in scented rain.
It is enough, ah wind, that I am living
And spring has tuned my harp to song again.

Lavender alliums float above an Illinois garden.
Photo by Jessie Walker.

Ideals' Family Recipes

When spring's flowers are at their peak and the air has lost its last chill, why not plan a garden brunch? These recipes are sure to please, whether you invite a few or a flock. Send Ideals *a typed copy of your favorite recipe along with your name, address, and phone number to* Ideals Magazine, 535 Metroplex Drive, Suite 250, Nashville, Tennessee 37211. *We will pay $10 for each recipe used.*

Favorite Breakfast Casserole

Madeline P. Kirby of Capron, Virginia

10 eggs
2 cups milk
2 teaspoons ground dry mustard
1 teaspoon salt
8 slices bread, cubed
1½ cups sharp Cheddar cheese, shredded
1 pound sausage, chopped and cooked

In a large bowl, beat together eggs, milk, mustard, and salt. Set aside. Arrange bread cubes in a greased 9-by-13-inch casserole. Top with cheese and cooked sausage. Pour egg mixture over bread mixture. Cover with plastic wrap and refrigerate overnight.

Preheat oven to 350° F. Bake 50 minutes or until casserole is puffed and set. Cut into squares. Makes 8 to 10 servings.

Zucchini Cakes

Phyllis M. Peters of Three Rivers, Michigan

2 cups peeled, shredded zucchini
⅓ cup biscuit mix
2 beaten eggs
¼ cup grated Parmesan cheese
Pepper to taste
Vegetable oil

In a large bowl, combine first 5 ingredients and mix well. Heat oil in large skillet over medium heat, using approximately 1 to 1½ tablespoons oil per patty. Drop batter by tablespoons into skillet. Brown cakes on both sides. Inside of cakes should remain moist. Cakes can be frozen and warmed in microwave. Makes approximately 12 cakes.

Best-Loved Oat and Applesauce Muffins
Margaret Anderson of Dunkerton, Iowa

1 cup all-purpose white flour	1 teaspoon baking soda	1 teaspoon vanilla
½ cup whole wheat flour	¼ cup oat bran	¼ cup vegetable oil
¼ cup brown sugar	1 cup quick-cooking oats	½ cup raisins
½ teaspoon nutmeg	2 eggs	Sunflower nuts
¼ teaspoon salt	¾ cup applesauce	Cinnamon
2 teaspoons baking powder	½ cup buttermilk	Granulated sugar

Preheat oven to 375° F. In a large bowl, sift together first 7 ingredients. Stir in oat bran and oats; set aside. In a medium bowl, beat eggs with fork. Stir in applesauce, buttermilk, vanilla, and oil. Mix well. Using a fork, slowly stir applesauce mixture into dry ingredients just until moistened. Fold in raisins. Spoon mixture into 16 large, greased muffin cups. Sprinkle with sunflower nuts, cinnamon, and sugar. Bake 20 minutes. Makes 16 muffins.

Herb Onion Bread
Margaret Anderson of Dunkerton, Iowa

3¼ cups all-purpose flour, divided	½ teaspoon ground sage	1 cup finely chopped onion
2 packages dry yeast	½ teaspoon crushed rosemary	1¼ cup warm water
2 tablespoons granulated sugar	¼ teaspoon ground thyme	1 egg
1 teaspoon salt	¼ cup butter	

In a large bowl, sift 1½ cups of flour with yeast, sugar, salt, sage, rosemary, and thyme. Set aside. In a small skillet, sauté onion in butter until golden; add to flour mixture. Add water and egg. Using an electric mixer, blend at low speed until moistened; beat an additional 3 minutes at medium speed. Using a large spoon, slowly stir in remaining flour to make a stiff dough. Spoon into a greased 2-quart casserole dish. Cover and let rise in a warm place until dough has doubled in size, approximately 1 hour.

Preheat oven to 375° F. Bake 35 to 40 minutes or until golden brown. Makes 1 loaf.

But only the

POWER OF BEAUTY

Mary O'Connor

My garden is like needlepoint today
With memory's embroidery on the edge.
Each flower's gentle messages portray
The sacredness of beauty like a pledge;
The birds come close, as faith has made
    them bolder,
And I can feel God smiling at my shoulder.

HILLTOP GARDEN

Rose Koralewsky

Coreopsis incredibly golden,
Great masses of cornflowers blue,
A velvety rose of deep crimson,
Alyssum of soft, pearly hue.

The infinite hills are around it,
The infinite heavens above.
I worship the hills and the heavens,
But only the garden I love.

The wind passeth over it, truly:
Its days are as grass—it is gone:
Yet somewhere in memory's pleasance
Each blossom, unfaded, blooms on.

*A stone wall fails to restrain this hillside garden in California.
Photo by Jessie Walker.*

The Garden of the Bees

Gene Stratton-Porter

There was something about the house shaded by tall eucalyptus trees and lacy jacqueranda, with its gaudy surrounding carpet of blue flower magic that gave to it, Jamie could think of no other term, a welcoming face. It seemed to be a human thing and it seemed to smile the warmest kind of welcome.

As he stood there looking down the stretch of the garden to the sea, he thought it comprised the most beautiful picture that he had ever seen. A crude walk, fashioned from stones collected from the mountainside, ran in steps down to the beach below. There was a pergola loaded with grapes as they are allowed to run in the gardens of the East, but lavishly among them grew wisteria and clematis, roses and vines whose names, habits, or flowering he did not know. On either hand, sometimes with abrupt juttings of big rocks, sometimes in tiny fertile plateaus, sometimes on gentle slopes, there grew every fruit tree that loves to flourish in the soil and sun of California— loquats and figs, oranges and lemons, plums and peaches, pears and nectarines, dates and grapefruit—only a tree or two of each, and between and beneath them tiny cultivated beds of vegetables.

Prominently bordering the walk halfway down the mountainside, staked and rankly growing, Jamie's eye was caught by a blare of purple-red where stalks of tomatoes lifted huge fruits, some of them bursting with ripeness, and on either hand everywhere, bushes, shrubs, vines and flowers, and flowers, and yet more flowers, and because Jamie recognized nearly each one of these, he knew they were the quaint, old-fashioned flowers that his mother and his grandmother had grown. . . . Carpeting around them were beds of cinnamon pinks, touching the fresh salt air with their spicy sweetness, mignonette and heliotrope, forget-me-nots and great blue blooms of myrtle the like of which Jamie never had seen—a whole world of flowers and fruit.

On either hand, steadily, slowly, came the low hum of millions of working bees—bees hived, not in the ugly flat houses used in numberless apiaries he had passed on his journey, but each stand in a separate spot raised above the earth on a low platform and having a round pointed roof that gave to the hives a beauty, a quaintness, an appropriateness to the location. On close examination Jamie found that each hive stood in a bed of myrtle blue as the sky. And then he saw that back of the hives the fences were a wall of the blue of plumbago, delicate sheets of it. And above, one after another, great lacy jacquerandas lifting clouds of blue to the heavens. And then he realized that, facing the hives, around and near them, there was a world of blue: blue violets, heliotrope, forget-me-nots, blue verbenas, blue lilies, larkspur, bluebells, phlox, blue vervain, blue and yet more blue. . . . It seemed as if the blue flowers dearly loved to creep up to these white hives, to vine around them, to cling to them, to bloom above them. . . .

There are only a few places where love and artisanship build a small house with a welcoming face. There are only a few places where love and good horse sense build a garden, . . . where the side of a mountain walks down, and slides down, and jumps down, and meanders winding, flowering ways until it reaches the white sands of a brilliantly blue sea, and it is easy to believe that such a location would naturally be the home of tiny round white houses with round roofs where millions of bees make honey to sweeten the food of a world.

Flowers tumble over stones and steps in A Sunlit Garden *by artist Pauline Delacroix-Garnier. Image from Christie's Images.*

Nancy Skarmeas

GENE STRATTON-PORTER

In the first decades of the twentieth century, few American writers were as widely read and enjoyed as Gene Stratton-Porter, author of such sentimental nature novels as *Freckles* and *Girl of the Limberlost*. In all, Stratton-Porter wrote fifteen novels; her books were read by an estimated fifty million Americans and translated into seven foreign languages. Avid readers were delighted and entertained by Stratton-Porter's works, yet she hoped they would also pause and consider the beauty and complexity of the natural world. The public clamored for more of her novels, but fiction was never Stratton-Porter's

top priority. She saw herself, first and foremost, as a naturalist. Whereas American society of the early twentieth century was more prepared to embrace a woman as a novelist than a scientist, it is as a naturalist that Gene Stratton-Porter deserves to be remembered today—as a woman who translated an intense love of nature into a lasting contribution to American natural history.

Geneva Stratton was born in 1863 on Hopewell Farm near Wabash, Indiana. Her mother was ill for many years and died when Geneva was twelve years old. Because of her mother's illness and early death, Geneva was raised mostly by her father and her eleven older siblings. Stratton-Porter later described her childhood: "Instead of 'sitting on a cushion and sewing a fine seam' as my sisters had, I spent my waking hours in the wild following my father and brothers to the field, amusing myself with birds, flowers, and insects." Indeed, while most girls of her generation were being raised to master the skills of homemaking, Geneva Stratton was learning to identify the birds and animals in the world outside the farmhouse. When she married Charles Porter in 1886, Geneva, or Gene as she was called by then, was ill-prepared and little inclined to become the conventional society wife that her husband's status as a successful businessman seemed to preordain.

Charles and Gene had one child, Jeanette. Stratton-Porter was a devoted mother who spent her days happily with her daughter in the family's home in the town of Geneva, Illinois. But when Jeanette was old enough to enter school, Gene Stratton-Porter was faced with a choice. Tradition called for her to devote her new-found time to the town's active social circles. But such a life held no appeal for her. Instead, Gene Stratton-Porter decided to rediscover the natural world that had so excited her as a child. During the hours while Jeanette was at school, she began exploring the local Limberlost Swamp, characterized by a writer of the day as "25,000 acres of treacherous swamp and quagmire filled with every plant, animal, and human danger." The ladies of the town looked askance at their neighbor and gossiped amongst themselves about her forays into the swamp; but Stratton-Porter was entranced by the world of the swamp. She began compiling nature studies and eventually, at the urging of her husband, submitted one in the form of an article to *Recreation* magazine. The piece was accepted, and Gene Stratton-Porter's career as a writer began.

Inspired by her first writing success, Stratton-Porter continued to write and submit nature study articles to magazines, with much success. After several years, she imagined that she could reach a broader range of readers if she transformed her observations on nature into fictionalized stories. She was successful at first try. She sold several short stories with nature themes to national magazines before an editor suggested that she expand her stories to book length. *The Song of the Cardinal* was Stratton-Porter's first novel. It was based entirely on her observations of birds in the Limberlost Swamp, but presented, and embraced by the public, as fiction. For nearly twenty-five years, Stratton-Porter would continue writing fiction and would become one of the most beloved authors of her generation.

But no matter what her success as a writer, Stratton-Porter would rather spend time tramping through the swamp and observing the life that teemed within. She was infinitely patient, able to win the trust of the birds and animals she studied and thus to record behaviors never before known to scientists. And she recorded not just with her pen, but with her camera. Early in her career, disappointed with the quality of illustrations offered for her writings, she began learning how to take her own photographs. Never one to do anything halfway, Stratton-Porter worked at her photography until she was as skilled with the camera as she was with the pen.

In the years that she was known throughout the world as a novelist, Stratton-Porter also published seven book-length nature studies describing the life of the Limberlost Swamp, studies that remain valuable scientific records to this day. Entirely self-trained, Stratton-Porter was nonetheless a firm believer in scientific method. Although other naturalists would publish conclusions based upon two sightings, she insisted upon at least a dozen sightings to verify any of her own conclusions. *Moths of the Limberlost* was one of her book-length nature studies, one which took twelve years of careful work to complete, twelve years of ignoring waist-deep mud, bug bites, and bee stings as she tracked these delicate and elusive swamp creatures of the Limberlost.

Gene Stratton-Porter was among our nation's earliest conservationists, becoming particularly vocal against the destruction of natural resources after Limberlost Swamp began to be drained for farmland in 1913. The destruction led her to find a new home—a woodland cabin on the shores of Sylvan Lake, where she continued her extraordinary research and writing. Still as active as ever in her seventh decade of life, Stratton-Porter died in an automobile accident in 1924, her life and work cut tragically short.

In today's world, where most girls are encouraged to pursue any dream or occupation, it is hard to imagine just how remarkable Gene Stratton-Porter was. Without a doubt, her body of work stands on its own merits and needs not be qualified as the achievement of a great *woman* writer and naturalist. But her decision to make such a life for herself does have everything to do with her being a woman. When Gene Stratton-Porter chose the swamp over the drawing room, when she chose a life pursuing what she loved rather than what was expected of her, she defied a powerful set of conventions.

Carrying a revolver as a defense against poisonous snakes, strapping a camera and tripod to her back, wearing leather hiking boots and a simple khaki skirt, Gene Stratton-Porter no doubt inspired gossip among the proper ladies of her town. As she set out in search of the secrets of nature, Stratton-Porter created something that would far outlive any idle gossip—she created a body of work that still serves as a valuable resource for scientists today; and she did this with the support of her husband and daughter, who often accompanied her as assistants during her forays into the wilderness. Her daughter once said of her mother, "Hers were such busy hands, they fluttered over everything, the velvet cheek of a baby, the down on a butterfly wing, the grain in a beautiful piece of wood." These busy hands were what allowed Gene Stratton-Porter to do what she loved, not what the world expected of her, thus making of her own life something extraordinary.

Nancy Skarmeas is a book editor and mother of a toddler, Gordon, who is keeping her and her husband quite busy at their home in New Hampshire. Her Greek and Irish ancestry has fostered a lifelong interest in research and history.

THE GENE STRATTON-PORTER STATE HISTORIC SITE
ROME CITY, INDIANA

Michelle Prater Burke

As a child, I spent many a happy hour playing house, or "treehouse," among the branches of a nearby pine grove. Piles of pine straw became beds, and pieces of bark were transformed into dinnerware. Days spent gathering pansies for my flower press or searching the woods for secret hideouts under drooping branches further introduced me to the wonders held by the outside world. Today, my leisure time is limited, and I more often search for lost car keys than woodland hideaways.

I did not realize how much I missed my early affinity with nature until recently when I visited the Gene Stratton-Porter State Historic Site near Rome City, Indiana. As I toured the log home known as "The Cabin in Wildflower Woods" and its vast gardens, I was inspired by how this famous author, naturalist, and photographer dedicated her life to the habitat surrounding her home and made the natural world her own.

Nestled on the shores of Sylvan Lake, where she had often visited as a child, the Gene Stratton-Porter State Historic Site encompasses the house, gardens, and wooded property where Stratton-Porter and her family made their home from 1914 until 1923. A flagstone path shaded by an arbor of wisteria leads to the log home made of Wisconsin cedar where I began my tour. The Cabin in Wildflower Woods was designed by Stratton-Porter and her husband and built in 1914 after they left their home near the Limberlost Swamp in Geneva, Indiana. I was not surprised to see the outside brought indoors in the native-stone fireplaces and the hand-rubbed, wild cherry paneling. In the author's study, where she penned such works as *Birds of the Limberlost* and *Michael O'Halloran*, the walls are filled with pho-

tographs and memorabilia from her lifetime of work.

Lovely as the home is, my eyes kept drifting through the windows to the gardens and forest outside, which were as much a home to the author as the cabin. The formal gardens encompass three-quarters of an acre and are composed of thirty-five garden plots, each maintained according to Stratton-Porter's original map and plant listings. The Porters planned their property to be the "garden spot of Indiana." As I later walked along the trim paths, I was surrounded by a portion of the three thousand wildflowers, shrubs, and trees Stratton-Porter transplanted from nearby areas that were being cleared. The gardens sit amid thirty-four acres of woodland, a portion of the property's original 150 acres of undeveloped forest, which once provided a rich source of material for Stratton-Porter's nature studies and photography. I eagerly joined a guided foray into the woods and was amazed by the variety of flora and fauna we encountered amid the tranquil scenery.

As I breathed in the pure air of the woods, I understood why Stratton-Porter had chosen the Wildflower Woods for her home and research and why she felt she had uncovered a paradise of sorts here in Indiana. She could have found no sweeter perfume than that of the flowers and no better art than that of a woodland butterfly. These are the joys which filled the days of this famous naturalist, and these are the wonders that once entranced me as a child. My visit to the shores of Sylvan Lake has inspired me to spend a little more time exploring the habitat around my own home. Once I find my old flower press, I plan to head to the garden in hope of discovering, just like Gene Stratton-Porter, all that nature has to offer.

The flagstone footpath and wisteria-laden arbor welcome visitors to the Gene Stratton-Porter State Historic Site.
Photo by Chuck Hine/Indiana Scenic Images.

Sweet Peas Bring Memories

Frances Carter Yost

Today I breathed the fragrance of sweet peas;
On wings of memory I flew to years
When I was wearing long pigtails with ease
And climbing fences with no sign of fears.

It was her wedding day, a girl named Dove,
Who lived next door, an idol in my eyes,
Grown tall and beautiful and now in love.
She called me from my work of fresh mud pies

To ask if I would gather flowers then.
Her dress was sweetheart necked with princess lines.
Would I pick flowers? Each last specimen!
My scissors snipped until (as fragrant shrines)

Exotic incense filled her bridal room;
Sweet peas bring memories each time they bloom.

Here are sweet peas, on tiptoe for a flight;

With wings of gentle flush o'er delicate white,

And taper fingers catching at all things,

To bind them all about with tiny rings.

—John Keats

This bouquet of sweet peas is beautiful enough for any bridal room. Photo by Carolyn Parker, FPG International.

My May Basket

Allie S. Van Scoik

A mysterious noise that is outside my door,
Oh, what can it be? I hear it once more.
Then, "May basket for you" in a childish voice sweet;
As I open the door, there's a scamper of feet.
A frisk and a rush as they flee out of sight,
And behold on my door is a May basket bright.

I lift it with care from its perilous place
And take it inside, my table to grace.
O sweet little basket, what treasures you hold,
More precious to me than silver and gold.
Spring beauties are there and adder-tongue too,
Buttercups sweet and violets so blue.

Dear little blossoms, you turn back the years
To childhood's glad time with its laughter and tears
And bring back to mind the days long ago
And teachers so kind with their faces aglow.
As they took from my hands these same treasures bright
That the children have left by my doorstep this night.

Though many dear friends from this earth are away,
And my locks that were brown are now threaded with gray,
Yet the years have rolled back and I wander once more
O'er the hillside and glen and their treasures explore.
O dear little basket, with your message of cheer,
I hope you will come to my door every year.

A basket of May blooms passes from garden to doorstep to tabletop. Photo by Nancy Matthews.

A crown of pink roses enthrones a simple wicker chair. Photo by David Noble/FPG International.

Mother's Rose

Mary Tortorice

Flowers blooming round the door
Make me think of Mother more.
Flowers grand and flowers small—
Mother knew and loved them all.

Cloistered near the garden gate
Bloomed a rose, a beauty late.
Queen of flowers, perfumed rare,
Mother always found it there.

Many times I've heard her say,
"Perhaps the rose will bloom today."
Choice of all her lovely flowers,
Standing tall through rain and showers.

Every year its joy it brought,
Gladly given to all who sought.
Mother's rose so choice and fair,
I hope to always find it there.

Violets, Daffodils

Elizabeth Coatsworth

Violets, daffodils,
Roses and thorn
Were all in the garden
Before you were born.

Daffodils, violets,
Green thorn and roses
Your grandchildren's children
Will hold to their noses.

My Mother's Garden

B. Hansen

Beneath the blaze of noon, gold lilies pose,
Incredible against the white stone wall
That guards its treasures well. A late blown rose,
Still queenly, holds two hummingbirds in thrall.

Blue larkspur casts soft shadow shapes to hide
Quaint pansy faces from the sun's caress.
The zinnias, never cold or dignified,
Outdo themselves this year with cheerful dress.

Great clumps of phlox send forth the faint, cool scent
My mother loved within the circled scheme.
The patient labor of her hands, intent
On giving, lives beyond her loving dream.

Green Melody

Jessie Cannon Eldridge

Life comes, turning every item
In its path to green once more.
Grass, as velvet as a carpet,
Is laid straightway to my door.
Tree leaves open as my heart does
From this sweet and warming thing.
Buds of flowers swell while singing
Songs of green. Oh, it is spring!

Little Leaves

Rose Koralewsky

The little leaves—I love them, every one:
The green hearts beating on the aspens tall,
The rosy parasols the maples spread,
The verdant flame-tips flickering on the birch,
The pink absurdities that grace the oak,
The tulips' dainty spades, the larches' ferns:
The whole wide world's one throbbing note of green!
Sun glances from each little burnished shield;
Wind makes a pattering as of tiny hands.
May days are beautiful, May nights are sweet,
Filled with the sight and sound of little leaves.

*Bunchberry flowers and gentian leaves create a rain-wet mosaic along
Alaska's Lynn Canal. Photo by Jeff Gnass Photography.*

Country CHRONICLE
Lansing Christman

THE LILACS OF MAY

Mother's Day comes at a lovely time of year: when Maytime lilacs bloom! As I take my evening walk, I see they are blossoming again along the old garden walls, and rows of them frame the dooryard lanes in purple and blue, lavender and white. How richly they bring the colors of the skies down to earth.

Lilac bushes have been my harbinger of May for many years. I know of some bushes that are much older than I am; and I have watched several generations of them come into bloom, just as my mother did for all of her springtimes.

My mother loved lilacs. I don't need the coming of May or lilac blooms to remember my mother, but I always associate their colorful displays with her and her passion for flowers. She enjoyed arranging colorful bouquets of blooms on tables and stands throughout our home; and in May, bunches of aromatic lilacs perfumed every corner of the house with their sweetness.

Always at this time of year, it is the fragrance of the lilac that lures me to sit for a while in the twilight hours and quietly enjoy that familiar aroma as it is carried on the gentle evening breeze. The dew makes even richer the fragrance of the flower.

I am glad that the cycle of the seasons continues and it is May again. In my reverie, as the stars begin to appear in the skies, my heart remembers my gingham-aproned mother and her love of flowers.

The author of three published books, Lansing Christman has been contributing to Ideals *for almost thirty years. Mr. Christman has also been published in several American, foreign, and braille anthologies. He lives in rural South Carolina.*

Photographer Gene Ahrens captures a perfect lilac bloom in Ringwood, New Jersey.

Mother Love

Janie Alford

I bent my ears to a lily's cup
And thought that it spoke to me,
By the stainless white of its petals light,
Of a mother's purity.

To the heart of a red, red rose I crushed,
And it seemed that within my eyes
There was shadowed the gleam of the crimson stream
Of a mother's sacrifice.

I considered the sun and the moon and the stars,
The winds and the tides of the sea
And found in the span of their beautiful plan
All a mother's constancy.

Then I lifted my eyes to a hilltop lone,
Where Love hung high on a tree.
And lo, it was there I could best compare
My mother's love for me!

A mother spends a quiet afternoon with her children in MRS. LEOPOLDINE MASARAI WITH HER DAUGHTERS AT THE ARTIST'S STUDIO by Hans Tichy (1861–1925). Image from Christie's Images.

Devotions
FROM THE Heart

Pamela Kennedy

And pray in the Spirit on all occasions with all kinds of prayers and requests. With this in mind, be alert and always keep on praying for all the saints. Ephesians 6:18 NIV

MOTHER'S PRAYERS

I was talking with another mother recently, and we were discussing our children. She has two sons who live far from home—one in college and one on his own. "Isn't it difficult," I asked, "to maintain that closeness you had when they were home?" She admitted it was at times, but then shared with me the secret of how she managed to still feel near to them.

"Every day, when I walk past their rooms or drive by the school they attended or the field where they played ball, I talk to God about them. Sometimes I ask Him to give them good friends or wisdom in making decisions or discernment at work. Just because they are far away doesn't mean I can't still be an influence in their lives."

Father, I thank You for children. Help me to remember that You love them even more than I, and that You desire to bless them beyond what I can hope or imagine. Help me to be faithful in prayer for them whether they are at home or away.

She had captured the essence of prayer as Paul expressed it in his letter to the believers at Ephesus. At all times, prayer keeps the hopes, praises, and concerns we have for those we love in the forefront of our minds and hearts.

But Paul enjoins us to not only pray at *all times*, but with *all kinds* of prayers. Some of us have been trained to think of prayer as primarily asking God for favors. We perceive a need, have an illness, experience fear or worry, and we're quick to fall on our knees to seek assistance for ourselves or those we love. What other kinds of prayers could Paul mean?

Scripture is filled with examples of different kinds of prayers. In the Psalms we read David's words praising God for His power and strength displayed in nature, in the affairs of men and women, in the tiny details of everyday life. The wisdom of God is another theme worthy of praise and is a primary focus of Solomon in his Proverbs. In both Old and New Testaments, prayers of thanksgiving are offered by people of faith. Hannah's prayer of gratitude after God blesses her with a son is echoed by Mary when she learns of her unique destiny. The prophets and apostles continually offer prayers of thanks for God's provision for their daily needs. Prayers in search of forgiveness and restoration of relationships fill the Bible as well. There is no scarcity of prayers—short, long, poetic, cryptic, seeking, offering—literally all kinds at all times.

We cannot always be with our children. Then we can pray for God to direct them. Our advice may not always be welcomed. Then we can pray for the Holy Spirit's influence to guide them. Our children may not be aware of how much they owe their heavenly Father. Then we can offer our prayers of praise on their behalf. We may have a broken relationship with our children. Then we can pray for God's grace to heal. Prayer is a powerful opportunity offered to each of us by the Lord. As mothers we have both the privilege and obligation to pray. We can remain close to our children in both heart and mind as we pray for them at *all times* with *all kinds* of prayers.

A favorite book is shared in WOMAN AND CHILD READING *by artist Kate Elisabeth Olver. Image from Christie's Images.*

HOUSE BLESSING

Arthur Guiterman

Bless the four corners of this house,
And be the lintel blest;
And bless the heart and bless the board
And bless each place of rest;
And bless the door that opens wide
To stranger as to kin;
And bless each crystal windowpane
That lets the starlight in;
And bless the rooftree overhead
And every sturdy wall.
The peace of man, the peace of God,
The peace of love on all!

PLAN FOR A NEW HOUSE

Grace Noll Crowell

Here on this little plot we will build our home.
The delicate lines of the blueprint cannot show
How deep the foundations will rest
    in the earth's good loam,
Nor how high in our hearts the lifted walls will go.
They cannot tell the beauty of morning light
Flooding a casement, nor of winds that run
Through open doors, nor translate sounds at night
Of eager feet on the sills, the day's work done.

Against the years and the storms we will build. The rock
Must be of the field, the carven oak and the pine
Will be a part of high hills, and sturdy the lock,
And tight be the roof, and the window glass must shine.
But the strength that runs forever
    through joists and beams
Is the immortal, ageless stuff that we call our dreams.

Flowers surround a welcoming cottage in Louisville, Kentucky.
Photo by Daniel Dempster.

Artist Diantha York Ripley captures the polished elegance of an old home in INSIDE INTERIOR. *Image from the collection of the artist/Diantha York Ripley/Superstock.*

One Old House

Janice Graham

This can't be it," I told my husband. "It's it," he said, parking our rental car in front of the once comfortably inviting yet formal English Tudor. "Three-twenty-six El Cerrito Avenue."

I couldn't believe it. For one thing, the seventy-foot-tall pine, perfect for climbing, had vanished. Jasmine, like a bulky sweater, replaced the sloping front lawn. The house itself had an altered look, painted a light gray-blue. In place of the distinctive crescent window at the house's pinnacle was a deck.

We climbed the same old brick stairs to the trumpet-vine covered path I used to

sweep. The solid front door seemed to be the same one, only now it bore a small glass window etched with a floral pattern. I remembered a time when it was all a little girl could do to pull the door open. I rang the bell, and a friendly lady in an apron answered.

"I used to live here," I blurted out. "I loved this house. Would you mind if we took a peak?" She seemed to understand and graciously treated us to a leisurely tour.

The house I remembered was open-armed and welcoming, a respite from the glare of a sometimes harsh, growing-up world. Solid and permanent seemed the massive oak dining set which it was my job to dust, the hardwood floors and muted Persian carpets, the wide, curving staircase, the large front hall where my sister and I had whirled round and round singing "Shall we dance?"

With a shock I saw that it was completely changed. But I had to admit the new tenants had done lovely things to the century-old house. They had lightened up walls and floors and remodeled and expanded rooms.

I was eager to see the kitchen where my mother had taught me to make bread from scratch and prepared for her wonderful dinner parties. Once flanked by an old-fashioned butler's pantry and generous back porch, the new room was now modernized beyond recognition. Even more remarkable were the changes in the sunken library with its leaded windows with diamond panes. The home's new owners had extended the room upward one full story and topped it with an elegant stained-glass ceiling. But to me it was still the room where I had often sat on my dad's lap in an old leather chair and listened to him read to me from the classics that lined the shelves.

On the first landing I was relieved to see, untouched, the polished hardwood corridor where my mother and I, tired from our chore of straightening the long row of ceiling-high closets, had once spontaneously taken a little nap together on the floor.

But it was my old room I most wanted to visit. When I was about eight years old, my father took me to a home furnishings store and let me choose my own carpet, wallpaper, and bedroom set. I knew exactly what I wanted: carpet the color of a tropical sea and wallpaper the same blue-green printed

> *I was relieved to see untouched the polished hardwood corridor where my mother and I, tired from our chores, had once spontaneously taken a little nap together on the floor.*

with country cottage scenes. I chose a canopy bed dressed in single-ruffled cloud white, a drop-leaf desk for stationery and sealing wax, and a six-drawer dresser. My room had a little walk-in closet which held my own sink and medicine chest, handy since the top floor had no bathroom.

But all I recognized of my perfect bedroom was its imposing window, really the best part, which still opened inward to reveal a view of redwood trees and housetops stretching to the far-off bay.

My husband and I peeked into the backyard on our way out. I was sure that at least the sprawling rose garden would still be growing. There my sister and I were once in charge of pruning all the faded blossoms. Hating to waste the soft, scented petals, we brought them in the house and, spreading them over the sheets, lay on our own wilted "bed of roses." But the roses were gone, along with the blackberries, the rabbit hutches, the trampoline under the magnolia tree, and the vegetable garden. In their place was a perfectly trimmed patio and garden and a guest house at a little distance, settled among the blossoming trees and sculptured greenery.

Physically, the old house was much changed, but its calm, good spirit was just the same. Elizabeth Goudge wrote, "How can we help loving houses when they stand for so much—warmth and protection and a means of expressing ourselves. You love a new house because it stands there waiting to be good to human beings and an old one because it has been." I came away from the house of my childhood feeling as if I had enjoyed an intimate visit with a refined, cultivated old friend. It had been good to me. And nothing can change that.

Chintzware

Sarah Niceley

When I was a girl of eight, my grandmother embarked on a trip to England. It seemed so wonderful to me, such an adventure. My grandfather had died a few years before, and Grandmother had resolved not to sit at home longing for the past. So she and a group of friends became travelers. They'd made their first trip to the West Coast, and then, their ambition growing, they crossed the Atlantic Ocean to visit England. I remember imagining my petite and soft-spoken grandmother exploring the streets and museums of London. I felt proud and excited, and I knew she was sure to bring me home something wonderful. And she did, although I didn't realize it at the time. The day after my grandmother's return, I waited anxiously as she gently lifted from her suitcase a package wrapped in brown paper and tissue. Inside was a teacup and saucer, both decorated with a pretty green floral pattern. Grandmother told me they were called chintzware, but I didn't pay much attention. I'd hoped for a one-of-a-kind toy; a teacup and saucer did little to inspire my imagination. But I thanked Grandmother and then placed the cup and saucer on my shelf, where they stayed throughout the remainder of my childhood.

When I left home, I packed the chintzware set away in a box of odds and ends, where it stayed for many long years. I had all but forgotten about the gift until I moved into my first house and came across the box holding Grandmother's cup and saucer. I unwrapped the set and put it on a shelf in my china cabinet. As the days and weeks passed, I began to see that old cup and saucer with new eyes. They were pretty, but not overly delicate, and the floral pattern felt like a breath of spring air even on the grayest of days. But most of all, that little teacup and saucer reminded me of Grandmother.

Today, my grandmother's teacup and saucer are the heart of my small but growing collection of chintzware—patterned, everyday pottery inspired by the colors and designs of a floral fabric known as chintz. I cannot rank myself among the most avid of collectors. I have seen pictures of homes where chintzware covers every available space, where the drapes and upholstery feature chintz patterns, where the effect is one of walking into a very profuse flower garden on a bright June day. My collection is more like a quiet floral oasis in the otherwise rather unremarkable decor of my home. I have all but filled that china cabinet where I first displayed grandmother's gift. I have a cream and sugar set made by the Royal Winton company in a pattern called Julia. I also have a wide variety of cups and saucers in floral patterns of every imaginable color. I look especially for tea sets, although I don't aim for complete sets; I just buy what catches my eye. I have purchased most of my chintzware here in America—in antique shops, at flea markets, at auctions, and lately over the internet. My greatest prize, however, I bought on my own first trip to England. I'd saved some money for the purpose of bringing home a truly special piece of chintzware. In a tiny antique shop in a little village not far from London, I found a Royal Winton Queen Anne Athena teapot. It was not inexpensive, but it is charming and beautiful, and it now occupies center stage on the shelf of my china cabinet.

I know exactly what it is that appeals to me about chintzware. I like the way that it is beautiful without being formal; chintzware is not so fine as to seem out of place in the casual decor of my home. And, certainly above all else, I love chintzware because of the association with my grandmother and that long-ago gift of a teacup and saucer. Instead of a toy that would soon be discarded or outgrown, Grandmother gave me a gift that has opened the door to a lifetime of simple pleasure. Every time I pause to look at the blooming colors inside my china cabinet, every time I find a particularly lovely piece of chintzware in an antique shop, I say a quiet thank you for her love and thoughtfulness.

NOT TOO CHINTZY

If you would like to collect chintzware, the following information will be helpful:

This chintzware stacking teapot and teapot/waterpot/tray set represent the Joyce-Lynn pattern. They were produced by Royal Winton on commission of Magnolia Antique Mall in El Cajon, California.

HISTORY

•Chintzware was inspired by colorful, printed and glazed fabrics of India called *chints*. The fabrics were imported into England in the seventeenth century and proved so popular that British parliament banned chints in 1722 to protect domestic fabric makers. In response, British weavers began making their own chintz fabrics. Not long after, English potteries began producing earthenware featuring chintz patterns.

•Early potteries producing chintzware in the eighteenth century included Chelsea, Wedgewood, Royal Worcester, and Doulton.

•The original chintzware was hand-painted and expensive. In the eighteenth century, the technique of transfer printing was developed, which simplified production and reduced prices. A century later, colored lithography further reduced the cost of chintzware. Thereafter, chintzware became affordable and popular throughout England.

•During the late nineteenth and early twentieth centuries, the English center for chintzware production was Stoke-on-Trent, in Staffordshire, which is north of London.

•Chintzware enjoyed a surge of popularity in the United States in the early 1980s after the wedding of Prince Charles and Princess Diana caused widespread interest in all things British.

COLLECTING

•There are two types of chintzware collectors. Some seek only antique pieces of chintzware, others are happy with recent reproductions.

•Chintzware items include tea sets, biscuit (cookie) jars, jugs, clocks, bowls, candlesticks, jam pots, and butter dishes.

•The most valuable chintzware is that which was manufactured in England between 1920 and 1960. Some potteries have recently reissued popular patterns made during that period.

•The most popular chintzware patterns include Julia, Summertime, Blue Chintz and Pink Chintz, Welbeck, and Stratford (which is quite rare).

•Collectors can authenticate a piece's origin by looking for the stamped name of the maker and for patterns with a recognizable history.

•Chintzware has been widely exported. Thus, collectors need not go to England to find pieces; they are available at antique shops and auctions throughout the United States.

Remember When

GIVE ME AN OLD-FASHIONED PEDDLER

Marjorie Holmes

In my hometown, each day stretched out before the housewife pretty much like the day before. She was glad to pause in her often horrendous labors (scrubbing on a washboard, say, or whaling the daylights out of a rug) and pass the time of day with a peddler while examining his wares. Those who came calling door-to-door—whether regulars like the Jewel Tea man and old blind Mr. Clarke, who sold soap, or the occasional stranger with brooms over his shoulder—were treated like welcome guests.

"Oh, my goodness, here comes the Jewel Tea wagon," my mother would exclaim. "Pick up those papers quick, and just look at this floor!"

Mr. Hix, the Jewel Tea man, didn't seem to notice, sitting at the oilcloth-covered kitchen table, drinking coffee, and passing along gossipy items picked up on his peregrinations, while Mother scribbled additional items on her list. We usually trailed him out to his "wagon," which was actually a skinny-wheeled, top-heavy truck. But, to our dazzled eyes and nostrils, its dusky interior, fragrant with spices, cocoa, tea, its air of plenitude and mobility, made it as enchanting as a desert caravan.

Mother, like many women, always had to rationalize what she bought. "Well, now yes, they are a little higher than the stores downtown, but it's so convenient. And they give such nice premiums."

The premiums were the payoff—the real forerunner of today's trading stamps. She was saving her coupons for a fringed floor lamp.

Another regular was Mrs. Cannon, a large, rich-smelling woman who took orders for yard goods, ribbons, and lace. We called her the Lace Lady; she always wore fountains of it at her wrists and throat, or a lacy shirtwaist tucked into a crackling taffeta skirt. The bolts of lace she brought forth from her big black leather satchel and unwound before your eyes—thick creamy ecru stuff for the yokes of nightgowns or the bordering of curtains and tablecloths; exquisite hand embroidery from the Philippines, or a delicate white froth, like snowflakes or spiderwebs.

The "goods" had to be ordered from her fabulous sample books. Children lived for the day when she would abandon one of these treasuries and pass it on. Their rectangles of precious satin, velvet, woolens, and gingham prints made marvelous dresses for the tiny penny dolls we bedded down in match boxes; and they couldn't be surpassed for curtaining and carpeting a shoebox dollhouse.

On a rare and memorable occasion we'd have a chimney sweep. Where they came from it's hard to imagine—Dickens? A fairy tale? Anyhow, one day a pair of them would appear, as if by magic, one on each side of the street. Elfish-looking little men in tall, pointed hats, their white smiles slashing their sooty faces, gay and a bit terrifying. They would go squirreling onto a roof and disappear into the chimney, probing and prodding with their devilish-looking instruments. The chimneys, clotted from years of wood and coal smoke, would rain down their velvety black accumulation.

Less spectacular but always diverting were the men who sharpened knives and scissors on their portable grinding wheels. And the genteel young ladies who took orders for the Book of Knowledge. Commonplace but perhaps jolliest of all were the broom peddlers.

"Brooms for sale . . . nice, new brooms!" the broom peddler would call, humping along under the burden of his heavy, bright bouquet. He carried them over his shoulder, those homely wheat-colored whiskery flowers. And what a fine business he did.

The money was counted out and the man trudged on. There you were with the new broom

A salesperson creates a welcome break from the day in this photograph from Superstock.

smelling dry and oaty, to be straddled and ridden, making a fine swish, and leaking a few loose golden strands across the floor.

Some things never change. We had then, as now, the perennial parade of small boys and girls selling seeds and postcards and subscriptions (and took our own exciting turns at the ringing of doorbells). Before long we began to have our Fuller Brush men, our Avon ladies, our assaults of young people "working their way" through college. Gradually, something began to be missing, there I'm sure as well as here in suburbia today; the flavor and juice of the old-time interruptions. The sense of

expectation, welcome, and surprise. But most of all, a sense of personal involvement with these briefly passing lives.

My children, however eager, can't really enjoy seeing me cope with all these people, as I proclaim in some desperation: "No, no, I cannot use any more brushes, beauty products, magazines, or cemetery lots."

I'd like to fling open the door some day and find a genuine blind man tapping up the steps. Or an old-fashioned smelly hobo to be fed and warmed and sent on his way . . . Or a lady with ribbons and laces . . . A peddler of brooms—a chimney sweep!

DOORBELLS

Isla Paschal Richardson

When my front doorbell rings and hurriedly
I answer on a busy day and see
A little neighbor child, there comes to me
A certain tender warmth. I stop and chat
About the kittens and the mother cat,
Of frogs and butterflies, and this and that;

Loving the upward glance, the eager word
That tells me how she found a baby bird,
Or of the cardinal that she had heard.
Sometimes I find an empty spool and soap
And we blow bubbles, or with microscope
We watch the anthills by the heliotrope.

I go back to my desk and know my smile;
My reason for this pause a little while
Is in remembering a low-built stile
I often crossed to reach a neighbor's door
(Of treasured memories my richest store!)
And ring her bell when I was only four.

MIRACLE SEEDS

Ruth E. Shaw

She rang my bell—a lovely child—
And as I answered, merely smiled
Then offered gaily pictured seeds,
All meant to fit my garden needs.
"A little late," I said, and yet
Chose cosmos, phlox, and mignonette.
I saw the roses in her cheeks,
Rare as any gardener seeks,
Soft eyes shining, heavenly blue,
That vied with morning glory hue.
She counted change and skipped away,
Leaving seeds of hope that day,
Sunshine too—enough to start
A flower garden in my heart.

A petite guest stops to chat in THE VISITOR *by artist Arthur Hopkins (1848–1930). Image from Christie's Images.*

A SLICE OF LIFE

Edgar A. Guest

A BABY IN THE HOUSE

Something to talk about, something to do,
Something to laugh at the whole day through,
Something to look at with pride and with glee,
Something for friends to come in just to see;
Oh, you can't sum up all the wonderful things
Of joy and delight which a new baby brings.

There's a smile that is brighter than sunbeams of May,
A wave of farewell as you're starting away,
A glad time of frolic which no one can steal,
A thrill inexpressible, lovely to feel.
There's something to boast of and something to tell
When a baby has come to the place where you dwell.

There's never an hour that is lonely and drear;
The days are filled up to the top with good cheer.
You have someone to play with and someone to sing to,
Someone to romp with and someone to cling to;
And always you're finding some pleasure that's new
When God has sent down a glad baby to you.

Edgar A. Guest began his illustrious career in 1895 at the age of fourteen when his work first appeared in the Detroit Free Press. *His column was syndicated in over three hundred newspapers, and he became known as "The Poet of the People."*

Her Faith

Esther F. Thom

"Bless Mother, Daddy too, Amen,"
She prayed beside her little bed.
"It's time to turn the lights down low,
Why are you kneeling still?" I said.

So simply she expressed her faith,
"Right now I'm listening quietly,
And waiting just to see if God
Has anything to say to me."

Nightly Quiz

LaVerne P. Larson

"Why is the world so big and round?
How high is the sky, how deep is the ground?
Could all of us fly if we had wings?
Does a bird say words whenever he sings?
Where does the sun go every night,
And why do the stars twinkle so bright?
How come you're big and I am so small?
I wish you were little and I were tall.
Does God always know when we're good or bad?
Can we make Him happy and make Him sad?
Will going to school make me smart?
How do you mend a broken heart?
Is the ocean wider than I can see?
How many fish are in the sea?
A sleepy, cute, little curlyhead
Expected answers before going to bed.

This flower-laden bedroom is sure to bring only the sweetest of dreams. Photo by Jessie Walker.

A patient seamstress created this teddy bear from twenty-eight pieces of Australian boiled wool.

TEDDY BEARS

Stella Nance

I have been sewing since I was a young girl. My mother had so many practical skills to pass on, and since I was an only child, she passed them on in full measure to me. I learned to sew and knit and quilt and do needlepoint; but it is sewing that has stayed with me. As a mother my sewing skills have served me well. I've helped make and mend the children's clothes; I've replaced buttons and secured weakened seams. I've made Halloween costumes and clothes for school plays. But what I've loved most of all has been making stuffed animals. I made them for

my children when they were babies; and in recent years, I've made them for my three grandchildren—stuffed dogs, elephants, monkeys, and, of course, teddy bears. Most of our children grew up with a special bear, handmade for them by Mom, and now each of the grandchildren has one too.

This spring I am again working on a teddy bear. But there is no new child in the family; this bear is for my oldest daughter. While she is busy with her two young children in her house just down the street, I am at work in the sewing room of my home. She knows I have been quite occupied lately and assumes I am creating more gifts for the grandchildren—I can't wait to surprise her, grown-up or not, with a special teddy bear just for her.

My daughter has loved teddy bears since childhood, when her cherished companion was a cinnamon-brown bear made by the Knickerbocker Toy Company. The bear was a gift from a great aunt who was very dear to our family. I never made my daughter another bear myself, for she always adored her Knickerbocker friend. He had a sweet, wide face; thick, plush fur; and moveable arms and legs. My daughter has several old photos of herself with Teddy, and even more fond memories. Teddy saw her through the first day of school when she was six, through nights away from home at summer camp, and through all the joys and trials of growing up. She even remembers having him on her bed in high school, although she was careful not to let her friends know! After that, the special old teddy bear disappeared, somehow lost during the days when childhood was closing its doors. It is this old bear that I have in mind as I work on a brand new teddy bear for my daughter. I have always felt a tinge of guilt that I never sewed a special bear for her as I did for my other three children, and I want to bring back all the fond memories of her childhood friend.

The process of making a fully-jointed teddy bear requires carefully written instructions and well-practiced sewing skills, but simpler bears can be made by those who are new to sewing. If making a teddy bear appeals to you, search out a pattern suited to your sewing skills and follow the directions to the letter. I poured through craft books until I found a bear that looked like my daughter's old Knickerbocker bear and have personalized it somewhat through my choice of fabric, eye color, and decorations. Teddy bears can be made with any variety of fur fabric, as well as cottons, velvets, calicos, or denims. I have chosen a thick-piled fur in the same cinnamon-brown of my daughter's childhood bear and two chocolate-brown, smooth buttons for the eyes. When the kids were young, they loved their soft bears, with bodies and heads stuffed with the fluffy material called kapok. These were meant to be snuggled with, to be taken to bed, to be tossed and dragged through childhood. By the time our kids outgrew their bears—or at least outgrew carrying them with them and sleeping curled up around them—they were flattened and matted and bald in spots. But the bear I am making for my daughter is intended for display on a shelf and will be stuffed with a dense variety of foam chips, packed full enough to make it stiff and poseable. I know my daughter loves teddy bears, but I don't imagine she will be inclined to drag it with her to the little league park or to the backyard barbecue.

The details of any handmade teddy bear are up to the pattern and to the individual craftsperson. When complete, bears can be dressed in doll clothes, handmade outfits, or left alone. There are bears dressed to look like celebrities, those attired in the colors of favorite sports teams, and those designed and dressed to resemble favorite storybook characters. I am opting for a simpler, more classic approach and am going to tie a red plaid ribbon around my bear's neck, just like the one that once adorned my daughter's beloved old Teddy. Other than that, this teddy will be all soft brown fur.

You would be hard pressed to find someone whose heart cannot be warmed by the sight of a teddy bear.

You would be hard pressed to find someone whose heart cannot be warmed by the sight of a teddy bear. The first teddy bears were created in the beginning of the twentieth century and inspired by a cartoonist's depictions of President Theodore Roosevelt's reluctance to shoot a bear cub while on a hunting trip. From its inception, the teddy bear's popularity has never waned. Almost every child has a teddy bear; almost every adult can remember one. They are a classic symbol of childhood—of the happy, warm, secure moments of earliest youth. That is what I hope to bring to mind with this gift to my daughter. I hope she will look upon this bear and remember her favorite old Teddy and the happiest days of her own young life. I am glad I am finally giving my daughter her own homemade bear. Belated as it is, it will carry a wordless and timeless message thanking her for always being my little girl.

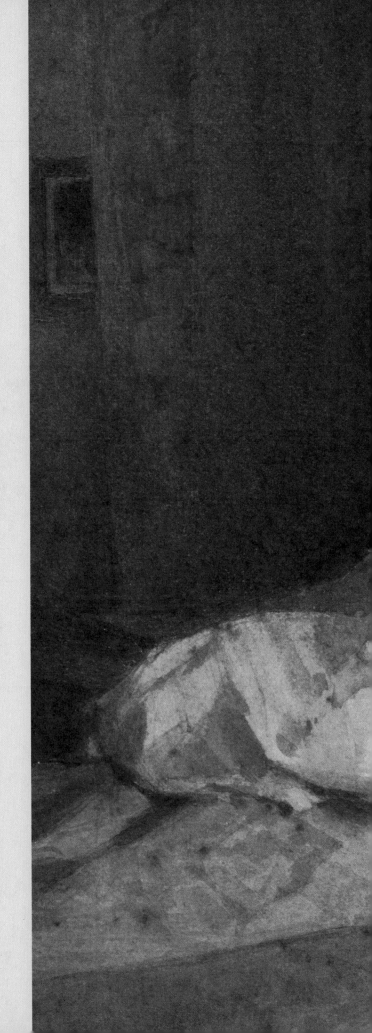

The Parallel

Betty W. Stoffel

My child is very young, so when he cries
At night, for fear of darkness or in pain,
My listening heart steals to his bed again,
And he can know my presence though his eyes
Can see me not in darkness where he lies.
The crying stops, the sobbings soon refrain;
I tiptoe out, but gifts of peace remain,
And then I pause, for parallel is wise:

Because my soul is young, it sometimes fears
The dark aloneness of its shadowed place.
Then God tiptoes beside me through the night—
I know He's there, though I see not His face.
And in His presence all is calm and right;
Because I am His child, I know He hears.

Peace I leave with you, my peace I
give unto you: not as the world giveth,
give I unto you. Let not your heart be
troubled, neither let it be afraid.

John 14:27

A mother smiles in wonder at her new child in A Mother with Her Baby
by artist Carlton Alfred Smith (1853–1946). Image from Christie's Images.

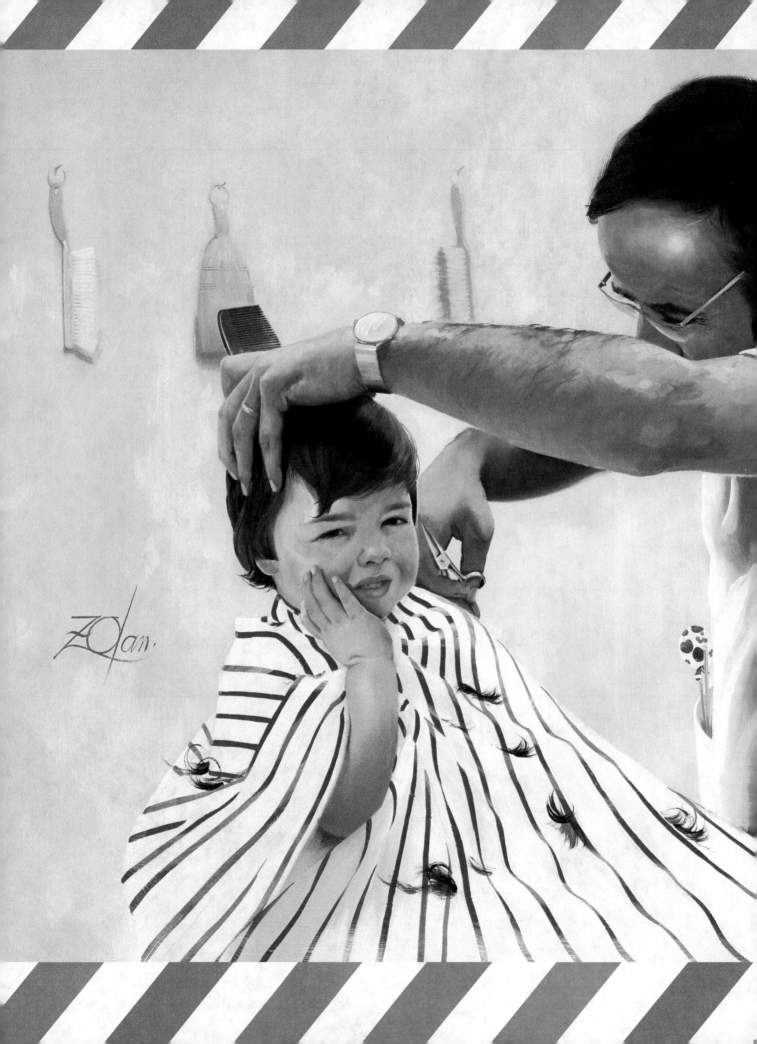

FOR THE CHILDREN

The Barber's

Walter de la Mare

Gold locks and black locks,
Red locks and brown,
Topknot to love-curl,
The hair wisps down.
Straight above the clear eyes,
Rounded round the ears,
Snip-snap and snick-a-snick
Clash the barber's shears.
Us, in the looking-glass,
Footsteps in the street,
Over, under, to and fro,
The lean blades meet.
Bay Rum or Bear's Grease,
A silver groat to pay—
Then out a-shin-shan-shining
In the bright, blue day.

A young boy has second thoughts in FIRST HAIRCUT *by American artist Donald Zolan. Copyright © Zolan Fine Arts Ltd., Hershey, Pennsylvania.*

Growing Time

Grace V. Watkins

A boy needs time to spend alone;
Sweet, precious hours for wandering through
A meadow, sitting on a stone
By little flowers, summer-blue.
A boy needs time for touching trees,
For listening to a brook that sings
In soft andantes and to bees
On sun-bright golden journeyings.
Oh, sometimes, gazing at the flow
Of gold and crimson in the gleam
Of sunset time, a boy will grow
Beyond what you can guess or dream.

A Small Boy's Pockets

Milly Walton

His bulging pockets yield so much
Of treasured loot preserved with care.
I gaze in wonder at each piece
To seek the magic he finds there.

A piece of glass to catch the sun,
An old bent nail, a knotted string,
A flat, white rock to skip the waves;
He sees some value in each thing.

A grubby penny for a sweet,
A stub of chalk, perhaps a snail,
A big blue taw still damp with earth,
A cancelled stamp from distant mail.

I cannot scorn the golden hoard
Within the pockets of a boy,
Each homely bit assumes a grace
Because it carried him some joy.

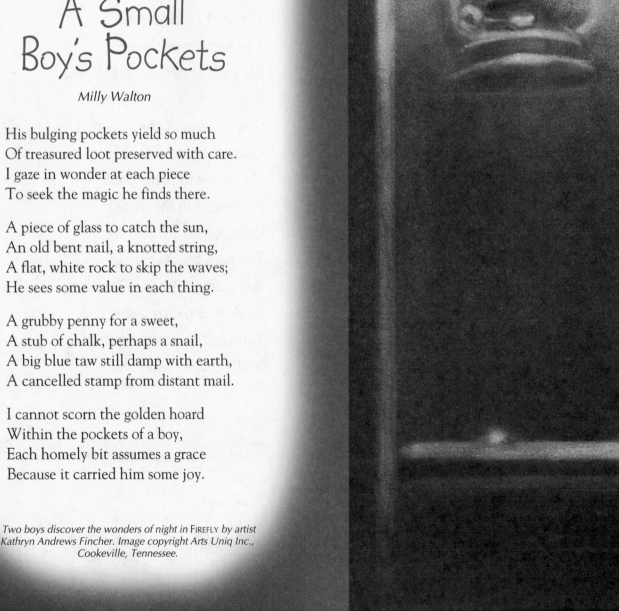

Two boys discover the wonders of night in Firefly *by artist
Kathryn Andrews Fincher. Image copyright Arts Uniq Inc.,
Cookeville, Tennessee.*

MY
GRANDDAUGHTER

Mary Roelofs Stott

In a traveled envelope
Came knocking the first photo
Of her, still so newly young.
She scarce can tell the brightness
Of the light in morning sun
From the darkness of the womb,
And still she knows the loving
That gives her place, she who never
Yet had been before in time,
Little stranger from afar.

And in her sighing content,
With tight clutch of minute hands,
Her smile's entering my heart
As I study the black hair,
So like mine when I was born,
And the face already shaped
Toward the woman she'll become.
And on my wall of pictures
I'm hanging hers at the top.

Ah, those glimpses framed and still,
From our wavering journey
Begun in shining and hope
With our darting sparks of mind.
And on sleepless nights of stars,
I can see my wall gleaming—
A ceremony of years
Stringing our chancing moments
In a living fire of grace.

SOMEWHERE

Marianne Miller

Somewhere in the past
lie the roots to
a legacy of love,
of faith and hope,
handed down through generations
of mothers.

Somewhere in the present
of everyday life
the thread continues,
weaving imperceptibly
the bonds that stretch forth,
reaching

Somewhere into the future
where the legacy grows,
keeping alive the mothers
who have gone before
for all the children
who are to come.

GENERATIONS

Georgia S. Cross

My child, the smile on your face
Will light a thousand faces
Like yours down through the ages.
Your child will wear your smile
And send it along
To his child, then on and on.
All the while,
Generations will wear your smile.

Old photos and books create a collage of memories in this photograph by Michael Mayor/FPG International.

Readers' Reflections

Mother
Leile Garber
Spokane, Washington

Paint her as you see her, artist.
Let the lines and wrinkles show;
And the silver hair that crowns her,
Make it like a halo's glow.

Can you picture on the canvas,
All the years of sacrifice,
How she tended all her household,
Ever counting not the price.

Let your brush tell the story
Of her patience, toil, and care.
Mingle love with joy and sorrow
Just as life has put them there.

Blend your colors softly, artist.
Face her toward the sun—
Smiling, calm, serene, and peaceful—
For her work is almost done.

Call the portrait simply Mother,
And the world will understand.
Nations thrive and emperors prosper
Guided by her gentle hand.

Dearest Mother
Pamela Clifton
Farmington, Missouri

I glanced into the mirror
and thought I saw you for a moment.
It was the same dark hair
and the same clear, penetrating eyes.
I had to turn away,
because I felt the tears come.
I stopped for a moment
as the memories came flooding back.
I heard your laugh,
and I saw your smile.
I felt your touch,
and I sensed your love;
And then I knew,
I was almost sure,
You had told me that you loved me.

Editor's Note: Readers are invited to submit unpublished, original poetry for possible publication in future issues of Ideals. Please send typed copies only; manuscripts will not be returned. Writers receive $10 for each published submission. Send material to Readers' Reflections, Ideals Publications, Inc., 535 Metroplex Drive, Suite 250, Nashville, Tennessee 37211.

Memories of Mother

Mary E. R. Herrington
Phoenix, Arizona

When I was just a little girl,
She spoke to me in quiet ways.
And with her gentle hand in mine,
How pleasant were my childhood days.

Each night we bowed our heads to pray
Upstairs beside the antique bed
To thank God for His many gifts,
Especially our daily bread.

Then ev'ry morn we knelt there too,
To thank God for a brand new day.
Mother taught us and always said,
"Things go better when you pray."

She helped me with so many things,
Especially when I went to school.

She said, "Work hard and doeth well,
And just obey the golden rule."

She taught me how to bake and sew
And how a sock with holes to mend,
That if someone should be in need
A helping hand we have to lend.

I still can hear her quiet voice
And see her sweet angelic face.
She had a way that was her own;
She brought love to the commonplace.

Though she's been gone a long time now,
Yet someday in that golden land,
I'll look and see that lovely face,
And once again I'll hold her hand.

No One Like Mother

Gail Elizabeth Newcomb
Aurora, Colorado

There's no other person
So sweet and so kind.
There's no other person,
At least in my mind,
Who cheers and brightens
The path being trod,
By smiling and winking
And giving a nod

Of encouraging strength
Through each trying day.
There's no other person
Who does it her way.
There's no other person,
No other you see.
There's no other person
Like Mother to me.

To an Adopted Child

Anne Campbell

Dear, do not weep! By every act of mine
I am your mother: by my sleepless nights,
By every step in the long day's design
That I have taken, by the sweet delights
Of your blest comradeship, by your clear gaze,
By all my care in your beginning days.

Your soft, warm body held against my breast
Warmed me and dried my disappointed tears.
You made a real home of our lonely nest.

Now we look forward to the fruitful years
With you beside us, bearing in your hands
The love that every mother-heart demands.

I am your mother; though you may not be
Flesh of my flesh, our love goes deeper still.
You are my heart's adopted, part of me.
I am your mother by the power of will.
Because I did not want to walk alone,
From the whole world I chose you for my own!

New Mother
of Two Adopted Children

May Smith White

She holds within her arms two golden gems.
Her hands will guide them through the days ahead,
And life will ring as true as olden hymns
As the story of this time will be reread.

The gleam of hope shown in her eyes today
Resolved my faith in youth's true motherhood.
And as I watched her walk this newer way,
I knew how deeply she now understood.

She once thought life replete with other things;
But then, she had not known of brighter springs.

A young child discovers a flower in this photograph by Superstock.

Lines of Tribute
for Mother's Day

Lucille Veneklasen

Her thoughtfulness and tenderness
Through all the years enduring;
Her quiet, spiritual steadfastness
So sweetly reassuring;

Her selflessness of soul which knows
Devotion's fullest measure;
The love a mother-heart bestows—
Earth's great abiding treasure.

My Mother

Elsie McKinnon Strachan

With gentleness she traced a living pattern
Of things to garner from life's unfolding field:
Among the careless weeds of words sown lightly
To seek the slender blade of truth's firm yield;
To read the message in November's snowflake;
To ponder frosted scenes etched on the pane;
To watch night snuff the flame of August twilight;
To smell the breath of April, fresh as rain;
To know no room is plain that wears fresh flowers,
Nor bare when furnished well with laughter's sound;
That kindness wears the cloak of thoughtful silence
Unless the spoken word is gently found.

The pattern that she traced stays with me yet,
Remembered well; this may I not forget.

A Life Poem
to My Mother

Agnes Davenport Bond

She left no poem for the world to read,
That is, she left no written words to tell
Her noble thoughts, her kindly acts and deeds.
But in the throbbing pulse of human life
There shone a brighter gleam of joy and hope,
Because that she had lived and loved mankind
And given of herself unselfishly.
Her life was just a poem in itself.
Not realized by those whom it had touched
So richly through the years, but living still
To spread its ray of gladness and of cheer
Within the hearts of all humanity.

*A treasured sketch of Mother offers a glimpse of the woman
she once was. Photo by Nancy Matthews.*

THROUGH MY WINDOW

Pamela Kennedy

Art by Pat Thompson

POST-DRAMATIC STRESS

When our two sons were teenagers, my husband attended skateboarding exhibitions, volleyball competitions, football scrimmages, and baseball games. He encouraged the boys by building ramps, playing catch, and discussing sports strategies. But when our daughter eschewed sports for the theater, my husband took off his ball cap, grinned at me, and said, "It's your turn, Mom!" I picked up the gauntlet. I'd make costumes, coach her on her lines, and sit appreciatively through amateur productions, beaming at my young thespian. It never occurred to me that I'd end up on the stage myself!

It happened during a community theater production of *The Music Man*. I drove her to the college campus where the auditions were being held and decided to accompany her into the building since it was several blocks from the parking lot, through wooded pathways. The director was a jovial fellow who welcomed everyone entering the room with a hug and an audition sheet. My protestations fell on deaf ears, and my daughter grinned. "Why don't you try out, Mom. You can sing okay, and you're going to have to drive me here and come pick me up anyway. Why not just stay and be in the ensemble." (Ensemble, I learned later, is a term for characters whose main function is to take up space.) Sparing all the details, let me just say that I did and I was.

Cast as a River City citizen, I should have realized right then and there that this would mean trouble with a capital "T"! At that point I didn't understand the basic premise of community theater: no matter how many roles there are, we'll fill them with whoever is here. Before the first week of rehearsals ended, I was not only a townsperson, but also a "Pick-a-Little" lady and one half of a supposedly adolescent couple in the "Shipoopie" dance number. That creative casting decision was made one evening when the director discovered he only had enough teenagers for seven couples and asked, in a booming voice, "Have any of you adults ever been to an aerobics class?" Innocently, I raised my hand (don't ever do this at a community theater unless you understand what you are volunteering for) and he shouted, "Great! You and Bill are now our eighth dance couple. Try to look like teenagers." I had just had my fiftieth birthday, and Bill was an insurance salesman with six kids. It was going to be a stretch!

As a resident of River City, I thankfully had few lines to memorize. Mostly I just moved with the crowd, except for the times when I forgot my blocking. I didn't have too much trouble with the songs, since I remembered most of them from the movie version when it was first released. What almost did me in, however, was the "Shipoopie." The choreographer envisioned this number as a raucous barn dance wherein the couples engaged in lots of hopping from side to side, skipping, kicking into the air, and do-si-doing. The problem was that this all had to be done in unison. While the light-footed teens bounced joyfully around their partners, Bill and I studiously muttered, "Right, left, right, right, right; left, right, left, left, left; hop one, hop two, hop three, kick!" It sort of took some of the bounce out of it. And then it didn't help when the director yelled from his perch in the lighting booth, "Okay, you kids take a break. Not you, geezer couple! Run that sequence again!"

We were finally getting the hang of things when the choreographer announced the addition of a lift to the dance. While I envisioned a public television special featuring the New York City Ballet, she continued.

"Here's what I want. All you guys run into the center, face out, and squat. Girls, run toward your partner, spin around, and jump backward into your partner's arms. Guys, grab the girls by the hips, lift them into the air, and run outward while you girls kick up your heels and squeal. Then girls jump down and go right into an allemande left. Got it?"

The teenaged girls were already squealing. I was contemplating having someone other than my husband "grab me by the hips" while I kicked up my heels! It was pretty tough to imagine. I glanced at Bill, who appeared to be rubbing a weak place in his lower back.

"Break!" yelled the director.

"Okay, Bill," I said, approaching him at the water fountain. "Here's the way I think it will work." And we discussed our strategy.

I got my husband to practice the lift with me in the living room at home until we had worked out a system where my weight was distributed more on his shoulders and chest than his back, and Bill trained by lifting sacks of peat moss using his legs. By the next dance rehearsal, we were at least not doing any permanent damage to ourselves and were keeping up with the younger couples, despite the fact that we still had to concentrate more and count under our breath.

By opening night, I was hitting my mark with precision, gossiping in time with all the other "Pick-a-Little" ladies, and managing to get through the entire "Shipoopie" number without flattening my partner. My husband attended at least a half a dozen performances, and he swears it wasn't just so he'd be on hand to call nine-one-one. In addition, my stock went way up with my daughter, who decided I was a pretty good sport—for a geezer.

Actually it was fun being in a production together. I cherish memories of nights when we drove home singing "Seventy-six Trombones" at the top of our lungs and laughing over some flub at rehearsal. But I have decided I wasn't cut out for a life in the theater—all the stress, the stage fright, the panic of a missed cue, a lost prop, a stuck zipper. Of course it was exciting too. And we did make lots of new and interesting friends. A few days ago, my daughter brought home a brochure announcing auditions for *The Sound of Music*, suggesting that we do another mother-daughter production. I told her I definitely wasn't interested. Of course, there are a lot of nuns in that one, and I'll bet they don't do any lifts.

Pamela Kennedy is a freelance writer of short stories, articles, essays, and children's books. Wife of a retired naval officer and mother of three children, she has made her home on both U.S. coasts and currently resides in Honolulu, Hawaii.

THE COOL GREEN MERE

Amy Carmichael

I see a little, cool, green mere
Like to a ruffled looking glass;
Where lovely, green lights interfere
Each with the other, and then pass
In rippled patterns to the grey
Of rocks that bar their further way.

I hear a mingled music now;
A streamlet that has much to tell,
And two sweet birds that on a bough
Near by love one another well.
And like a flake of summer sky
A pale blue butterfly floats by.

A sudden sun-flash and below,
Upon a rock of amber-brown,
Bright golden sparkles come and go,
As if in their dim water town
Set on that lighted pedestal,
The water things held carnival.

The mountain wind blows in my face,
I see the water, smell the rain,
Yet I am here in mine own place
With duties thronging me again;
But the more welcome, the more dear,
Because of you, my cool, green mere.

Oregon's Latourell Falls creates its own green mere in this photograph by Walt Puciata/Gnass Photo Images.

OUR HERITAGE

THE NINETEENTH AMENDMENT TO THE CONSTITUTION

Passed by Congress June 4, 1919
Ratified August 18, 1920

Section 1. The right of the citizens of the United States to vote shall not be denied or abridged by the United States or by any State on account of sex.

Section 2. Congress shall have power to enforce this article by appropriate legislation.

ABOUT THE TEXT

In 1920, Congress passed the Nineteenth Amendment to the Constitution and granted American women the right to vote. The ratification of the amendment in August of that year followed seventy-two years of organized struggle. The struggle began in July of 1848 when three hundred women and men, led by Susan B. Anthony, Lucretia Mott, and Elizabeth Cady Stanton, gathered in Seneca Falls, New York, for the first women's rights convention. The Seneca Falls Convention launched a passionate fight that, after more than seven decades, culminated in the Nineteenth Amendment and suffrage rights for mothers and daughters across the nation.

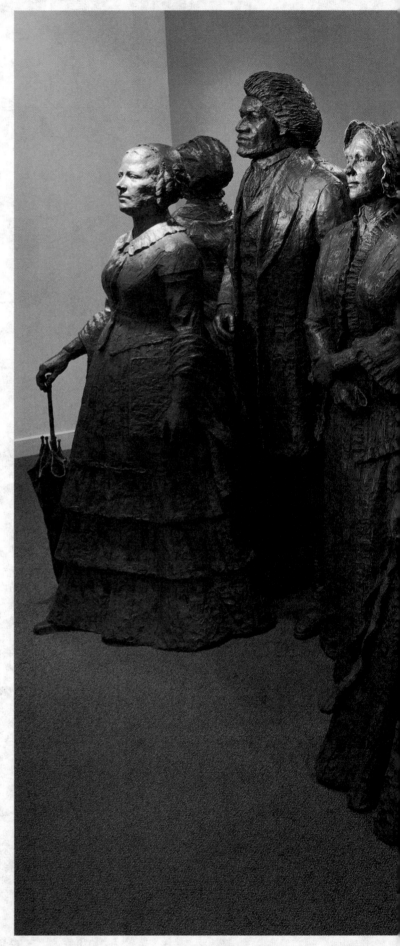

At the Women's Rights National Historical Park in Seneca Falls, New York, a bronze sculpture depicts the attendees at the first women's rights convention. Photo by Jeff Gnass.

"We hold these truths to be self evident:
that all men and women are created equal..."

Green Rain

Dorothy Livesay

I remember long veils of green rain
Feathered like the shawl of my grandmother—
Green from the half-green of the spring trees
Waving in the valley.

I remember the road
Like the one which leads to my grandmother's house,
A warm house, with green carpets,
Geraniums, a trilling canary
And shining horse-hair chairs;
And the silence, full of the rain's falling
Was like my grandmother's parlor
Alive with herself and her voice, rising and falling—
Rain and wind intermingled.

I remember on that day
I was thinking only of my love
And of my love's house.
But now I remember the day
As I remember my grandmother.
I remember the rain as the feathery fringe of her shawl.

A grandmother passes on her knowledge and her love in THE FIRST SEWING LESSON *by artist Frederick Daniel Hardy (1826–1911). Image from Christie's Images/Superstock.*

Act One

Josephine Powell Beaty

This evening will not come again,
And so I hold it to my heart.
These children playing on the lawn
Tomorrow morning must depart.

"Next summer," says my smiling son,
"I'll come and bring them back again."
But well he knows and so do I
They will be different children then.

For Time will lay its hands on them
And bend their spirits to its mold;
And they will lose that artless grace,
The magic of a three-year-old.

But now they scamper in and out
And reach on tiptoes for the skies
To try to catch and bring to me
Unwary, hapless fireflies.

And when at last the chase is won
With squeals of joy and rapturous hugs
They press into my outstretched hands
Some small, bedraggled lightning bugs.

Then darkness comes to halt their sport,
Reluctantly to bed they creep.
Excepting for the nursery light,
The world is plunged in silence deep.

Their footsteps cease; I hear again
The echo of their good-night call
And sit alone upon the lawn
To watch the curtain slowly fall.

But patience and another June
I will awake some happy morn
To listen with contented heart
To four-year-olds upon the lawn!

*Two generations share a walk in the orchard in this photograph by
Telegraph Colour Library/FPG International.*

May

Gladys Taber

The first time I went to the Metropolitan Museum in New York, I was so overcome by the riches that I felt faint. I managed to bear it until I got to the El Greco, and then I sat down trembling, and when I could get up again I went right down to the basement and had a pot of nice ordinary tea and a pedestrian, rather stiff, sandwich. For the truth is there is a limit to how much excitement one human being can endure.

I feel the same way about May, when apple blossoms cloud the air, tulips and narcissi bloom, violets are thick enough to walk on, and the lilacs lean above the white picket fence heavy with fragrance. May would be a wonder, I think, with just one blossoming apple tree or one small white lilac. Or one violet plant with purple blooms and heart-shaped, dark leaves. I would like to be able to play a lute and sit in the dappled shade and sing the hours away. However, I cannot carry a tune and the only instrument I ever could play was the ukulele, except for a brief struggle to master the guitar. So the music just stays in my heart.

It's time to get out the picnic basket and follow the footsteps of spring down the green valley and up the far hills. The tumbling brook, fringed with fern, skips over jeweled stones. The children used to make collections of the smooth ones—rosy, silvery, greenish. We'd take sandwiches and jugs of coffee and milk and sit on a flat gray ledge; while the children waded in the swift water, Jill and I would dream of making a wildflower garden in a smooth place at the brook's bend.

The garden never materialized, for leisure was hard to come by, what with raising all our vegetables, canning and freezing them, mowing a half-acre lawn, and taking care of cocker puppies and, during the war, eighteen laying hens.

I am a great believer in dreaming. Once you feel satisfied that everything is just so, you narrow your horizon. This is a far cry from not enjoying what you have. It just means not being static. Even an unrealized dream may be a blessing.

One of our dreams was realized, but it didn't just happen. There was a desiccated corncrib in the yard when we bought Stillmeadow. It was one-third full of rotting corn. We decided that where the crib stood would make a lovely quiet garden. Very simply, too.

First, it took a week to lug out the corn. . . . Then we had to hire a man to cut down the main beams because we couldn't lift them. And then we were left with the sorriest mess of rubble and mouse nests you ever saw.

It took days to clean all this up, after which we got a load of flagstones to lay in the middle of the garden and then hired Mr. Clark to put up a picket fence. After that, it took Jill about three years to reclaim the soil, get bulbs started, and plant roses and a lily-of-the-valley bed.

Like most hopeful gardeners, we put in too much, too close together, so Jill had to spend more time moving things out! But when the day came that we had some cedar furniture in the garden and ate our first lunch under the flowering crab, I said happily, "And to think this didn't cost anything."

"Just a gift," said Jill.

Lilacs are in bloom; on the old well house, wisteria begins to open amethyst buds. I am dazzled by all I see, but perhaps best of all I like the slope above the pond, where the daffodils and narcissi that Jill planted shine like countless gold and white stars. Again I ask myself, is this the same countryside that only a few months ago was swept by bitter winds? Or did I only imagine the stinging snow and glittering icicles? Changing seasons will forever be a mystery to me. Time has folded winter away into yesterday; tomorrow, summer will make May just a memory.

An old wagon bed becomes a backdrop for crabapple blossoms near Gastonia, North Carolina. Photo by Norman Poole.

The Hummingbird

Stella Craft Tremble

Beyond the rim of thought on silver wings
Vibrating in the glow of glistening things,
A hummingbird, like evanescent light,
Gleams iridescent in its shimmering flight.
A spinning flower on honeysuckle vine,
A flickering sheen above a columbine,
A whirring resonance and dart of blue
That stirs the very heart and soul of you.
A heavenly envoy on ethereal wings,
It fuses temporal and eternal things.

To a Hummingbird

Della Crowder Miller

Thou pretty, vibrant, humming thing,
Perpetual motion on the wing.
Your iridescent colors bring
Rare beauty to the twilight spring
As you, in your adventuring
For garden sweets, go foraging.
Sipping, darting, poising, seeming
Mystery of color gleaming.
You bring us heaven with your strumming
As through the twilight you go humming.

A female ruby-throat hummingbird feeds on scarlet sage in North Carolina. Photo by Norman Poole.

From My Garden Journal

Deana Deck

ALLIUMS

I'm sure you never considered giving your mother a bouquet of onion blossoms for Mother's Day, but you may soon change your mind as I did. A number of years ago I found myself enjoying the mild early-spring weather as I traveled through New York's Ulster County with a good friend. We drove down into a charming river valley between the Catskill and Shawangunk Mountains, and we entered a small agricultural community whose name has long escaped me.

From one horizon to another were fields composed of the blackest dirt I'd ever seen, and the entire village smelled like onions. The highway turned out to be the main street of town, and as we slowly drove along, taking in the sights, I spied a small house with a garden that seemed to have been planted by Martians.

The plants lining the picket fence were tall, some as tall as I am, and were topped by huge purple globes of some sort that

bobbed to and fro in the breeze like fuzzy party balloons. We drove on in amazement and soon discovered that nearly every house we passed had similar plants in the garden. Some were only two or three feet tall, but many were of the giant proportions we had first seen. All were topped by the same purple, fuzzy globes, like some over-anxious dandelions gone to seed.

I had no idea what plant I was viewing. Finally, I couldn't stand it a moment longer and asked that my friend stop the car in front of one of the homes where a woman was on her knees, pulling weeds. In response to my inquiry, she informed me that the plants were alliums. I'd never heard of them. She told me they are sort of like an onion and that we were in the heart of New York's onion-growing country, which explained the onion scent wafting on the breeze. Something about the soil, apparently—pitch-black, rich, and friable—was perfect for growing onions and all things related. Those related things included not only the spectacular ornamental plants known as alliums, but the entire amaryllis family, of which both onions and garlic are proud members.

As soon as I got home I pulled out the garden catalogs and started looking for alliums. Strangely enough, I had a hard time finding them, but that was twenty-five years ago. Today, thanks to their growing popularity and the ever-expanding nursery industry, alliums are more widely available, not only from mail-order nurseries but at local nurseries and garden centers and even home stores that sell bulbs in autumn.

Although directly related to the onion (*Allium cepa*), the ornamental garden allium that looks so foreign

ALLIUM

does not usually have the pungent smell of its cousins. On the contrary, the blooms of many are sweetly fragrant. There are hundreds of allium species. In fact, *Hortus Third*, a scholarly botanical encyclopedia, devotes four pages of tiny, single-spaced type to describe allium varieties.

Luckily, you don't have to plow through all that information to find a species that will do well in your garden, especially if you live in the temperate zones of the United States. A cool weather plant, alliums are a boon for northern gardeners and do not tend to thrive south of Zone 7. And for those who lose their tulip and lily bulbs to the bunnies, deer, and squirrels, there is good news: most wild critters turn their noses up at allium bulbs.

There is an allium to suit every garden, since the species runs the gamut from exceedingly tall to diminutive. *A. giganteum* is one of the tallest allium species, but it doesn't produce the largest blooms. That honor goes to a variety known as *A. Globemaster*.

But not all alliums are gigantic, nor are they all purple. There is dainty little *A. cyaneum*, for example, a sky blue, ten-inch tall variety that is popular for rock gardens. The *A. flavum*, which seldom grows more than twelve inches, produces lustrous yellow, pendulous blooms in the summertime. Another species, the perennial *A. Schoenoprasum*, produces pink blooms in spring and is better known to herb gardeners as chives. And *A. karataviense* is as popular for its hosta-like foliage as for its four-inch globes of red-purple blossoms.

So when it is time to arrange a bouquet for Mom, you have many choices. Alliums, many of which bloom around Mother's Day, make lovely cut flower arrangements. They do best if cut when only two-thirds open. Their seedheads are also attractive in dried arrangements, but plants dead-headed before going to seed will produce larger bulbs the following season.

> There is an allium to suit every garden, since the species runs the gamut from the exceedingly tall to the diminutive.

Alliums and onions prefer the same growing conditions. The village where I first spotted them is in a valley that is wall-to-wall bottom land. The small river that once filled the valley receded long ago, leaving thick layers of rich alluvial sediment.

Lots of sunshine and copious quantities of compost and manure will keep your allium garden thriving. So will fairly constant moisture; this is not a drought-loving plant. Once the blooms and foliage die back in summer, watering can be decreased, but during periods of active growth they need at least a half-inch of water per week. Some growers supplement nutrients with bulb food, and some advocate use of composted sewage sludge, sold in many communities for fertilizer. Milorganite is one of the best known brands of this type fertilizer. It is produced by the Milwaukee water treatment plant and sold nationally.

Allium bulbs do not take up much space in the garden and can be planted profusely among perennials in the border. Because the allium foliage tends to wither and fade before the blooms mature, the foliage of other plants provides a valuable disguise. Blue *A. caeruleum* looks gorgeous planted among the peonies; and the Star of Persia (*A. Christophii*), with its masses of amethyst blooms, is an excellent companion for yarrow. Or perhaps try adding a few white, star-shaped *A. Napolitanum Cowanii* to a bed of Siberian iris.

I learned a valuable lesson the day I discovered alliums. It's simply this: don't be shy about pulling over to the side of the road to ask a gardener for information about his or her plants. You'll usually be exceedingly glad you did. Where else could I have found an out-of-this-world bouquet for Mother's Day?

Deana Deck tends to her flowers, plants, and vegetables at her home in Nashville, Tennessee, where her popular garden column is a regular feature in The Tennessean.

UPON RETURNING

May Smith White

Is this the lane where lilacs used to bloom—
Or have I missed the road that once I knew?
As here above the fence, no longer loom
The wind-blown lilacs I had longed to view.
For years, I somehow knew I would come back,
Although a silent voice had said to me:
Old scenes will be subdued, in some way lack
The beauty known upon each hill and lea.

But yet, I know I will return again
To claim a dream before it fades and dies;
To see a greening hillside washed in rain
And soon the clearness of the cobalt skies.
I will return again I know—I know—
To walk remembered paths of long ago.

FOOTPRINTS OF THE YEARS

Agnes Davenport Bond

Implanted in the depths within my heart
Are footprints of the years which I have known.
These memories, with which I would not part,
Are plainly traced like carvings on a stone.
Like baby footprints left in hard cement,
Which later on bring gladness mixed with tears,
So, too, the joys and sorrows time has lent
Are treasured in my breast through passing years.

The shadows that have fallen on my ways,
Which seemed so dark and brooding when they fell,
Have served to glorify the brighter days
And added something vital, too, as well.
Unwittingly life's footprints mark their prime
Upon the ever-moving wings of time.

Lilacs edge a well-worn path in South Berwick, Maine. Photo by William Johnson/Johnson's Photography.

Daylight's Last Call

Richard Williams

In the lengthening shadows of late afternoon,
The sun is a hesitant pallid balloon;
Its brief scarlet blush on the low western sky
Is all that remains as the evening draws nigh.
The valleys and hillocks, their woodlands and streams
Immerse in a purple-mist fabric of dreams.
Sounds become muted; the night-seeds are sown;
With solitude's urging, the shadows have grown.
Quiet expectancy looms like a wall,
An orphaned reminder of daylight's last call.

The Garden of Dreams

Bliss Carman

My heart is a garden of dreams
Where you walk when day is done,
Fair as the royal flowers,
Calm as the lingering sun.
Never a drought comes there,
Nor any frost that mars,
Only the wind of love
Under the early stars,
The living breath that moves
Whispering to and fro,
Like the voice of God in the dusk
Of the garden long ago.

A girl lights her lantern in preparation for a garden party in CARNATION, LILY, LILY ROSE (DETAIL) *by John Singer Sargent (1856–1925). Image from Tate Gallery, London/Bridgeman Art Library/London/Superstock.*

BITS & PIECES

The sunbeams dropped their gold and, passing
in porch and niche,
Softened to shadows, silvery, pale, and dim,
As if the very Day paused and grew Eve.
—Edwin Arnold

When day is done, and clouds are low,
And flowers are honey-dew,
And Hesper's lamp begins to glow
Along the western blue;
And homeward wing the turtle-doves,
Then comes the hour the poet loves.
—George Croly

The moon pull'd off her veil of light,
That hides her face by day from sight
(Mysterious veil, of brightness made,
That's both her lustre and her shade),
And in the lantern of the night,
With shining horns hung out her light.
—Samuel Butler

Th' approach of night,
The skies yet blushing with departing light,
When falling dews with spangles decked the glade,
And the low sun has lengthened ev'ry shade.
—Alexander Pope

Carry your own lantern, and
you need not fear the dark.
—Proverb

God shall be my hope,
My stay, my guide, and
lantern to my feet.

—William Shakespeare

Sweet shadows of twilight! how calm their repose,
While the dew drops fall soft in the breast of the rose!
How blest to the toiler his hour of release
When the vesper is heard with its whisper of peace!

—Oliver Wendell Holmes

Let no rash hand invade these sacred bowers,
Irreverent pluck the fruit, or touch the flowers;
Fragrance and beauty here their charms combine,
And e'en Hesperia's garden yields to mine.

—Author Unknown

It is the hour when from the boughs
The nightingale's high note is heard;
It is the hour when lover's vows
Seem sweet in every whispered word;
And gentle winds, and waters near,
Make music to the lonely ear.
Each flower the dews have lightly wet,
And in the sky the stars are met.

—George Gordon, Lord Byron

How lovely are the portals of the night,
When stars come out to watch the daylight die.

—Thomas Cole

Readers' Forum

Snapshots from Our Ideals Readers

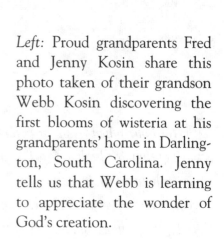

Right: Nancy Phan of South Amherst, Ohio, sent *Ideals* this snapshot of her three-year-old niece, Danielle Oziak. Nancy tells us that Danielle loves to come for a visit, and one of her favorite things to do is to help her "Aunt Nanny" plant beautiful flowers.

Left: Proud grandparents Fred and Jenny Kosin share this photo taken of their grandson Webb Kosin discovering the first blooms of wisteria at his grandparents' home in Darlington, South Carolina. Jenny tells us that Webb is learning to appreciate the wonder of God's creation.

Thank you Nancy Phan, Cheryl Scott, Dorothy Heckt, and Fred and Jenny Kosin for sharing your family photographs with *Ideals*. We hope to hear from other readers who would like to share snapshots with the *Ideals* family. Please include a self-addressed, stamped envelope if you would like the photos returned. Keep your original photographs for safekeeping and send duplicate photos along with your name, address, and telephone number to:

Readers' Forum
Ideals Publications, Inc.
535 Metroplex Drive, Suite 250
Nashville, Tennessee 37211

Above: Three-year-old Melanie Heckt proudly displays her freshly picked dandelion bouquet. This photo was sent to us by Melanie's doting grandma, Dorothy Heckt, who lives in Minneapolis, Minnesota.

Right: Cheryl Scott of Vancouver, British Columbia, shares this snapshot of her daughter, Katelyn Florence, gathering an armful of lilac blossoms. Cheryl tells us that Katelyn is her "little flower ever blooming."

Dear *Ideals*,

I have subscribed to *Ideals* since the first issue of December 1944 and hope to continue. It is the greatest publication, and I have given a number of subscriptions to different people in the past years. I have every copy and would not take anything for them.
Please keep up the good work!

LAURA MCKETTRICK
AUGUSTA, GEORGIA

Dear *Ideals*,

With every issue of *Ideals*, I quickly turn to the pages with the adorable pictures that are submitted from the readers. I am submitting the above picture of our black labrador retriever, Pearl. My husband, Mark, is training her and is very pleased with her progress. Of course, my job is to spoil her with treats and supply her with her favorite items: crushed ice and breadsticks—what a combination!

JACQUELINE M. SHORNAK
HOPEWELL, VIRGINIA

ideals

Publisher, Patricia A. Pingry
Editor, Michelle Prater Burke
Designer, Travis Rader
Copy Editor, Elizabeth Kea
Contributing Editors, Lansing Christman, Deana Deck, Pamela Kennedy, and Nancy Skarmeas

ACKNOWLEDGMENTS

CARMICHAEL, AMY. "The Cool Green Mere" from *Mountain Breezes* by Amy Carmichael, © The Dohnavur Fellowship, published by Christian Literature Crusade. Used by permission. COATSWORTH, ELIZABETH. "Violets, Daffodils." Reprinted with the permission of Simon & Schuster Books for Young Readers, an imprint of Simon & Schuster Children's Publishing Division from *The Littlest House* by Elizabeth Coatsworth. Copyright 1940 MacMillan Publishing Company; copyright renewed © 1968 Elizabeth Coatsworth Beston. CROWELL, GRACE NOLL. "Plan for a New House" from *Between Eternities* by Grace Noll Crowell, Copyright © 1944, renewed © 1972 by Reid Crowell. Reprinted by permission of HarperCollins Publishers, Inc. DE LA MARE, WALTER. "The Barber's" from *The Complete Poems of Walter de la Mare*. The Literary Trustees of Walter de la Mare, and the Society of Authors as their representative. GUITERMAN, ARTHUR. "House Blessing" from *Death and General Putnam and 101 Other Poems* by Arthur Guiterman. Reprinted by permission of Louise H. Sclove. HOLMES, MARJORIE. An excerpt from "Give Me an Old-Fashioned Peddler" from *You and I and Yesterday* by Marjorie Holmes. Reprinted by permission of the author. KORALEWSKY, ROSE. "Hilltop Garden" and "Little Leaves" from *New England Heritage* by Rose Koralewsky. Reprinted by permission of Branden Publishing. RICHARDSON, ISLA PASCHAL. "Door Bells" from *Along the Way* by Isla Paschal Richardson. Reprinted by permission of Branden Publishing. STOFFEL, BETTY. "As the Heart Remembers Spring" and "The Parallel" from *Moments of Eternity* by Betty Stoffel. Reprinted by permission of E. L. Stoffel. TABER, GLADYS. An excerpt from "May" from *The Stillmeadow Calendar: A Countrywoman's Journal* by Gladys Taber, Copyright © 1967 by Gladys Taber. TREMBLE, STELLA CRAFT. "The Hummingbird" from *The Crystal Prism*. Reprinted by permission of Trueman Tremble. YOST, FRANCES CARTER. "Sweet Peas Bring Memories" from *While Orchids Bloom* by Frances Carter Yost. Reprinted by permission of Rosalie Yost Roberts. Our sincere thanks to the following authors whom we were unable to locate: Josephine Powell Beatty for "Act One," Agnes Davenport Bond for "Footprints of the Years," Anne Campbell for "To an Adopted Child," Dorothy Livesay for "Green Rain," Milly Walton for "A Small Boy's Pocket," Grace V. Watkins for "Growing Time," and May Smith White for "Upon Returning."